Cover and page design by Julie Paillin. Each one of our publications takes time and effort to put together, if you enjoyed this please leave a review on Amazon. For more information on this and other titles go to jandspublications.com or email hello@jandspublications.com.We welcome all feedback, if there is anything you would like to see included in future editions please get in touch.

Enjoy!

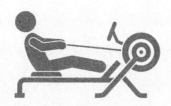

Row

Date: 23/9/24   Time: 16:00 AM/PM

Pre-Training Feeling: Weak   Not 100% ✓ Normal   Good   Strong

Distance: 8978   SPM: 22

Time: 45   500m/Split:

Intervals: —

Comments: first sessn of wp L3

Weight: Seasons Best   Personal Best

Post-Training Feeling: Tired ✓ Achy ✓ Proud ✓ Happy   Hard fun

Ski

Date: 24/9/24   Time: 5:45 (AM)/PM

Pre-Training Feeling: Weak ✓ Not 100%   Normal   Good   Strong

Distance: 8x500 4km SPM: 38

Time: 500m/Split: 2:26

Intervals: 8x500 č 2 min recovery

Comments: felt tired aftr yesterday's session

Weight: Seasons Best   Personal Best

Post-Training Feeling: Tired ✓ Achy ✓ Proud   Happy   Hard fun

Date: Time: AM/PM

Pre-Training Feeling: Weak   Not 100%   Normal   Good   Strong

Distance: SPM:

Time: 500m/Split:

Intervals:

Comments:

Weight: Seasons Best   Personal Best

Post-Training Feeling: Tired   Achy   Proud   Happy   Hard fun

---

Date: Time: AM/PM

Pre-Training Feeling: Weak   Not 100%   Normal   Good   Strong

Distance: SPM:

Time: 500m/Split:

Intervals:

Comments:

Weight: Seasons Best   Personal Best

Post-Training Feeling: Tired   Achy   Proud   Happy   Hard fun

Date: _____ Time: _____ AM/PM

Pre-Training Feeling: Weak   Not 100%   Normal   Good   Strong

Distance: _____ SPM: _____

Time: _____ 500m/Split: _____

Intervals: _____

Comments: _____

Weight: _____ Seasons Best _____ Personal Best

Post-Training Feeling: Tired   Achy   Proud   Happy   Hard fun

---

Date: [____] Time: [____] AM/PM

Pre-Training Feeling: Weak ☐ Not 100% ☐ Normal ☐ Good ☐ Strong ☐

Distance: [____] SPM: [____]

Time: [____] 500m/Split: [____]

Intervals: [____]

Comments: [____]
[____]

Weight: [____] Seasons Best [____] Personal Best [____]

Post-Training Feeling: Tired ☐ Achy ☐ Proud ☐ Happy ☐ Hard fun ☐

Date: Time: AM/PM

Pre-Training Feeling: Weak   Not 100%   Normal   Good   Strong

Distance: SPM:

Time: 500m/Split:

Intervals:

Comments:

Weight: Seasons Best   Personal Best

Post-Training Feeling: Tired   Achy   Proud   Happy   Hard fun

---

Date: Time: AM/PM

Pre-Training Feeling: Weak ☐   Not 100% ☐   Normal ☐   Good ☐   Strong ☐

Distance: SPM:

Time: 500m/Split:

Intervals:

Comments:

Weight: ☐   Seasons Best ☐   Personal Best ☐

Post-Training Feeling: Tired ☐   Achy ☐   Proud ☐   Happy ☐   Hard fun ☐

Date: Time: AM/PM

Pre-Training Feeling: Weak   Not 100%   Normal   Good   Strong

Distance: SPM:

Time: 500m/Split:

Intervals:

Comments:

Weight: Seasons Best   Personal Best

Post-Training Feeling: Tired   Achy   Proud   Happy   Hard fun

---

Date: Time: AM/PM

Pre-Training Feeling: Weak ☐   Not 100% ☐   Normal ☐   Good ☐   Strong ☐

Distance: SPM:

Time: 500m/Split:

Intervals:

Comments:

Weight: ☐   Seasons Best ☐   Personal Best ☐

Post-Training Feeling: Tired ☐   Achy ☐   Proud ☐   Happy ☐   Hard fun ☐

Date: Time: AM/PM

Pre-Training Feeling: Weak   Not 100%   Normal   Good   Strong

Distance: SPM:

Time: 500m/Split:

Intervals:

Comments:

Weight: Seasons Best   Personal Best

Post-Training Feeling: Tired   Achy   Proud   Happy   Hard fun

---

Date: Time: AM/PM

Pre-Training Feeling: Weak   Not 100%   Normal   Good   Strong

Distance: SPM:

Time: 500m/Split:

Intervals:

Comments:

Weight: Seasons Best   Personal Best

Post-Training Feeling: Tired   Achy   Proud   Happy   Hard fun

Date: Time: AM/PM

Pre-Training Feeling: Weak   Not 100%   Normal   Good   Strong

Distance: SPM:

Time: 500m/Split:

Intervals:

Comments:

Weight: Seasons Best   Personal Best

Post-Training Feeling: Tired   Achy   Proud   Happy   Hard fun

---

Date: Time: AM/PM

Pre-Training Feeling: Weak   Not 100%   Normal   Good   Strong

Distance: SPM:

Time: 500m/Split:

Intervals:

Comments:

Weight: Seasons Best   Personal Best

Post-Training Feeling: Tired   Achy   Proud   Happy   Hard fun

Date: _____ Time: _____ AM/PM

Pre-Training Feeling: Weak   Not 100%   Normal   Good   Strong

Distance: _____ SPM: _____

Time: _____ 500m/Split: _____

Intervals: _____

Comments: _____

Weight: _____ Seasons Best   Personal Best

Post-Training Feeling: Tired   Achy   Proud   Happy   Hard fun

---

Date: [____] Time: [____] AM/PM

Pre-Training Feeling: Weak [ ]   Not 100% [ ]   Normal [ ]   Good [ ]   Strong [ ]

Distance: [____] SPM: [____]

Time: [____] 500m/Split: [____]

Intervals: [____]

Comments: [____]
[____]

Weight: [ ] Seasons Best [ ] Personal Best [ ]

Post-Training Feeling: Tired [ ]   Achy [ ]   Proud [ ]   Happy [ ]   Hard fun [ ]

Date: Time: AM/PM

Pre-Training Feeling: Weak   Not 100%   Normal   Good   Strong

Distance: SPM:

Time: 500m/Split:

Intervals:

Comments:

Weight: Seasons Best   Personal Best

Post-Training Feeling: Tired   Achy   Proud   Happy   Hard fun

---

Date: Time: AM/PM

Pre-Training Feeling: Weak   Not 100%   Normal   Good   Strong

Distance: SPM:

Time: 500m/Split:

Intervals:

Comments:

Weight: Seasons Best   Personal Best

Post-Training Feeling: Tired   Achy   Proud   Happy   Hard fun

Date: Time: AM/PM

Pre-Training Feeling: Weak   Not 100%   Normal   Good   Strong

Distance: SPM:

Time: 500m/Split:

Intervals:

Comments:

Weight: Seasons Best   Personal Best

Post-Training Feeling: Tired   Achy   Proud   Happy   Hard fun

---

Date: Time: AM/PM

Pre-Training Feeling: Weak   Not 100%   Normal   Good   Strong

Distance: SPM:

Time: 500m/Split:

Intervals:

Comments:

Weight: Seasons Best   Personal Best

Post-Training Feeling: Tired   Achy   Proud   Happy   Hard fun

Date: Time: AM/PM

Pre-Training Feeling: Weak   Not 100%   Normal   Good   Strong

Distance: SPM:

Time: 500m/Split:

Intervals:

Comments:

Weight: Seasons Best   Personal Best

Post-Training Feeling: Tired   Achy   Proud   Happy   Hard fun

---

Date: Time: AM/PM

Pre-Training Feeling: Weak   Not 100%   Normal   Good   Strong

Distance: SPM:

Time: 500m/Split:

Intervals:

Comments:

Weight: Seasons Best   Personal Best

Post-Training Feeling: Tired   Achy   Proud   Happy   Hard fun

Date: _____ Time: _____ AM/PM

Pre-Training Feeling: Weak   Not 100%   Normal   Good   Strong

Distance: _____ SPM: _____

Time: _____ 500m/Split: _____

Intervals: _____

Comments: _____

Weight: _____ Seasons Best _____ Personal Best _____

Post-Training Feeling: Tired   Achy   Proud   Happy   Hard fun

---

Date: _____ Time: _____ AM/PM

Pre-Training Feeling: Weak   Not 100%   Normal   Good   Strong

Distance: _____ SPM: _____

Time: _____ 500m/Split: _____

Intervals: _____

Comments: _____

Weight: _____ Seasons Best _____ Personal Best _____

Post-Training Feeling: Tired   Achy   Proud   Happy   Hard fun

Date: _____ Time: _____ AM/PM

Pre-Training Feeling: Weak   Not 100%   Normal   Good   Strong

Distance: _____ SPM: _____

Time: _____ 500m/Split: _____

Intervals: _____

Comments: _____

Weight: _____ Seasons Best   Personal Best

Post-Training Feeling: Tired   Achy   Proud   Happy   Hard fun

---

Date: _____ Time: _____ AM/PM

Pre-Training Feeling: Weak ☐ Not 100% ☐ Normal ☐ Good ☐ Strong ☐

Distance: _____ SPM: _____

Time: _____ 500m/Split: _____

Intervals: _____

Comments: _____

Weight: _____ Seasons Best ☐ Personal Best ☐

Post-Training Feeling: Tired ☐ Achy ☐ Proud ☐ Happy ☐ Hard fun ☐

Date: Time: AM/PM

Pre-Training Feeling: Weak   Not 100%   Normal   Good   Strong

Distance: SPM:

Time: 500m/Split:

Intervals:

Comments:

Weight: Seasons Best   Personal Best

Post-Training Feeling: Tired   Achy   Proud   Happy   Hard fun

---

Date: Time: AM/PM

Pre-Training Feeling: Weak   Not 100%   Normal   Good   Strong

Distance: SPM:

Time: 500m/Split:

Intervals:

Comments:

Weight: Seasons Best   Personal Best

Post-Training Feeling: Tired   Achy   Proud   Happy   Hard fun

Date: Time: AM/PM

Pre-Training Feeling: Weak   Not 100%   Normal   Good   Strong

Distance: SPM:

Time: 500m/Split:

Intervals:

Comments:

Weight: Seasons Best   Personal Best

Post-Training Feeling: Tired   Achy   Proud   Happy   Hard fun

---

Date: Time: AM/PM

Pre-Training Feeling: Weak   Not 100%   Normal   Good   Strong

Distance: SPM:

Time: 500m/Split:

Intervals:

Comments:

Weight: Seasons Best   Personal Best

Post-Training Feeling: Tired   Achy   Proud   Happy   Hard fun

Date: _____ Time: _____ AM/PM

Pre-Training Feeling: Weak   Not 100%   Normal   Good   Strong

Distance: _____ SPM: _____

Time: _____ 500m/Split: _____

Intervals:

Comments:

Weight: _____ Seasons Best _____ Personal Best

Post-Training Feeling: Tired   Achy   Proud   Happy   Hard fun

---

Date: [_____] Time: [_____] AM/PM

Pre-Training Feeling: Weak ☐ Not 100% ☐ Normal ☐ Good ☐ Strong ☐

Distance: [_____] SPM: [_____]

Time: [_____] 500m/Split: [_____]

Intervals: [_____]

Comments: [_____]
[_____]

Weight: [____] Seasons Best [____] Personal Best [____]

Post-Training Feeling: Tired ☐ Achy ☐ Proud ☐ Happy ☐ Hard fun ☐

Date: Time: AM/PM

Pre-Training Feeling: Weak   Not 100%   Normal   Good   Strong

Distance: SPM:

Time: 500m/Split:

Intervals:

Comments:

Weight: Seasons Best   Personal Best

Post-Training Feeling: Tired   Achy   Proud   Happy   Hard fun

---

Date: Time: AM/PM

Pre-Training Feeling: Weak   Not 100%   Normal   Good   Strong

Distance: SPM:

Time: 500m/Split:

Intervals:

Comments:

Weight: Seasons Best   Personal Best

Post-Training Feeling: Tired   Achy   Proud   Happy   Hard fun

Date: Time: AM/PM

Pre-Training Feeling: Weak   Not 100%   Normal   Good   Strong

Distance: SPM:

Time: 500m/Split:

Intervals:

Comments:

Weight: Seasons Best   Personal Best

Post-Training Feeling: Tired   Achy   Proud   Happy   Hard fun

---

Date: Time: AM/PM

Pre-Training Feeling: Weak ☐   Not 100% ☐   Normal ☐   Good ☐   Strong ☐

Distance: SPM:

Time: 500m/Split:

Intervals:

Comments:

Weight: Seasons Best   Personal Best

Post-Training Feeling: Tired ☐   Achy ☐   Proud ☐   Happy ☐   Hard fun ☐

Date: Time: AM/PM

Pre-Training Feeling: Weak   Not 100%   Normal   Good   Strong

Distance: SPM:

Time: 500m/Split:

Intervals:

Comments:

Weight: Seasons Best   Personal Best

Post-Training Feeling: Tired   Achy   Proud   Happy   Hard fun

---

Date: Time: AM/PM

Pre-Training Feeling: Weak   Not 100%   Normal   Good   Strong

Distance: SPM:

Time: 500m/Split:

Intervals:

Comments:

Weight: Seasons Best   Personal Best

Post-Training Feeling: Tired   Achy   Proud   Happy   Hard fun

Date: Time: AM/PM

Pre-Training Feeling: Weak   Not 100%   Normal   Good   Strong

Distance: SPM:

Time: 500m/Split:

Intervals:

Comments:

Weight: Seasons Best   Personal Best

Post-Training Feeling: Tired   Achy   Proud   Happy   Hard fun

---

Date: Time: AM/PM

Pre-Training Feeling: Weak   Not 100%   Normal   Good   Strong

Distance: SPM:

Time: 500m/Split:

Intervals:

Comments:

Weight: Seasons Best   Personal Best

Post-Training Feeling: Tired   Achy   Proud   Happy   Hard fun

Date: Time: AM/PM

Pre-Training Feeling: Weak   Not 100%   Normal   Good   Strong

Distance: SPM:

Time: 500m/Split:

Intervals:

Comments:

Weight: Seasons Best   Personal Best

Post-Training Feeling: Tired   Achy   Proud   Happy   Hard fun

---

Date: Time: AM/PM

Pre-Training Feeling: Weak   Not 100%   Normal   Good   Strong

Distance: SPM:

Time: 500m/Split:

Intervals:

Comments:

Weight: Seasons Best   Personal Best

Post-Training Feeling: Tired   Achy   Proud   Happy   Hard fun

Date: Time: AM/PM

Pre-Training Feeling: Weak   Not 100%   Normal   Good   Strong

Distance: SPM:

Time: 500m/Split:

Intervals:

Comments:

Weight: Seasons Best   Personal Best

Post-Training Feeling: Tired   Achy   Proud   Happy   Hard fun

---

Date: Time: AM/PM

Pre-Training Feeling: Weak   Not 100%   Normal   Good   Strong

Distance: SPM:

Time: 500m/Split:

Intervals:

Comments:

Weight: Seasons Best   Personal Best

Post-Training Feeling: Tired   Achy   Proud   Happy   Hard fun

Date: Time: AM/PM

Pre-Training Feeling: Weak   Not 100%   Normal   Good   Strong

Distance: SPM:

Time: 500m/Split:

Intervals:

Comments:

Weight: Seasons Best   Personal Best

Post-Training Feeling: Tired   Achy   Proud   Happy   Hard fun

---

Date: Time: AM/PM

Pre-Training Feeling: Weak   Not 100%   Normal   Good   Strong

Distance: SPM:

Time: 500m/Split:

Intervals:

Comments:

Weight: Seasons Best   Personal Best

Post-Training Feeling: Tired   Achy   Proud   Happy   Hard fun

Date: Time: AM/PM

Pre-Training Feeling: Weak   Not 100%   Normal   Good   Strong

Distance: SPM:

Time: 500m/Split:

Intervals:

Comments:

Weight: Seasons Best   Personal Best

Post-Training Feeling: Tired   Achy   Proud   Happy   Hard fun

---

Date: Time: AM/PM

Pre-Training Feeling: Weak   Not 100%   Normal   Good   Strong

Distance: SPM:

Time: 500m/Split:

Intervals:

Comments:

Weight: Seasons Best   Personal Best

Post-Training Feeling: Tired   Achy   Proud   Happy   Hard fun

Date: Time: AM/PM

Pre-Training Feeling: Weak   Not 100%   Normal   Good   Strong

Distance: SPM:

Time: 500m/Split:

Intervals:

Comments:

Weight: Seasons Best   Personal Best

Post-Training Feeling: Tired   Achy   Proud   Happy   Hard fun

---

Date: Time: AM/PM

Pre-Training Feeling: Weak ☐ Not 100% ☐ Normal ☐ Good ☐ Strong

Distance: SPM:

Time: 500m/Split:

Intervals:

Comments:

Weight: Seasons Best   Personal Best

Post-Training Feeling: Tired ☐ Achy ☐ Proud ☐ Happy ☐ Hard fun

Date: Time: AM/PM

Pre-Training Feeling: Weak   Not 100%   Normal   Good   Strong

Distance: SPM:

Time: 500m/Split:

Intervals:

Comments:

Weight: Seasons Best   Personal Best

Post-Training Feeling: Tired   Achy   Proud   Happy   Hard fun

---

Date: Time: AM/PM

Pre-Training Feeling: Weak ☐   Not 100% ☐   Normal ☐   Good ☐   Strong ☐

Distance: SPM:

Time: 500m/Split:

Intervals:

Comments:

Weight: ☐   Seasons Best ☐   Personal Best ☐

Post-Training Feeling: Tired ☐   Achy ☐   Proud ☐   Happy ☐   Hard fun ☐

Date: Time: AM/PM

Pre-Training Feeling: Weak   Not 100%   Normal   Good   Strong

Distance: SPM:

Time: 500m/Split:

Intervals:

Comments:

Weight: Seasons Best   Personal Best

Post-Training Feeling: Tired   Achy   Proud   Happy   Hard fun

---

Date: Time: AM/PM

Pre-Training Feeling: Weak   Not 100%   Normal   Good   Strong

Distance: SPM:

Time: 500m/Split:

Intervals:

Comments:

Weight: Seasons Best   Personal Best

Post-Training Feeling: Tired   Achy   Proud   Happy   Hard fun

Date: Time: AM/PM

Pre-Training Feeling: Weak   Not 100%   Normal   Good   Strong

Distance: SPM:

Time: 500m/Split:

Intervals:

Comments:

Weight: Seasons Best   Personal Best

Post-Training Feeling: Tired   Achy   Proud   Happy   Hard fun

---

Date: Time: AM/PM

Pre-Training Feeling: Weak   Not 100%   Normal   Good   Strong

Distance: SPM:

Time: 500m/Split:

Intervals:

Comments:

Weight: Seasons Best   Personal Best

Post-Training Feeling: Tired   Achy   Proud   Happy   Hard fun

Date: _____ Time: _____ AM/PM

Pre-Training Feeling: Weak   Not 100%   Normal   Good   Strong

Distance: _____ SPM: _____

Time: _____ 500m/Split: _____

Intervals: _____

Comments: _____

Weight: _____ Seasons Best   Personal Best

Post-Training Feeling: Tired   Achy   Proud   Happy   Hard fun

---

Date: [_____] Time: [_____] AM/PM

Pre-Training Feeling: Weak ☐   Not 100% ☐   Normal ☐   Good ☐   Strong ☐

Distance: [_____] SPM: [_____]

Time: [_____] 500m/Split: [_____]

Intervals: [_____]

Comments: [_____]
[_____]

Weight: [__] Seasons Best [__]   Personal Best [__]

Post-Training Feeling: Tired ☐   Achy ☐   Proud ☐   Happy ☐   Hard fun ☐

Date: Time: AM/PM

Pre-Training Feeling: Weak   Not 100%   Normal   Good   Strong

Distance: SPM:

Time: 500m/Split:

Intervals:

Comments:

Weight: Seasons Best   Personal Best

Post-Training Feeling: Tired   Achy   Proud   Happy   Hard fun

---

Date: Time: AM/PM

Pre-Training Feeling: Weak   Not 100%   Normal   Good   Strong

Distance: SPM:

Time: 500m/Split:

Intervals:

Comments:

Weight: Seasons Best   Personal Best

Post-Training Feeling: Tired   Achy   Proud   Happy   Hard fun

Date: Time: AM/PM

Pre-Training Feeling: Weak   Not 100%   Normal   Good   Strong

Distance: SPM:

Time: 500m/Split:

Intervals:

Comments:

Weight: Seasons Best   Personal Best

Post-Training Feeling: Tired   Achy   Proud   Happy   Hard fun

Date: Time: AM/PM

Pre-Training Feeling: Weak   Not 100%   Normal   Good   Strong

Distance: SPM:

Time: 500m/Split:

Intervals:

Comments:

Weight: Seasons Best   Personal Best

Post-Training Feeling: Tired   Achy   Proud   Happy   Hard fun

Date: Time: AM/PM

Pre-Training Feeling: Weak   Not 100%   Normal   Good   Strong

Distance: SPM:

Time: 500m/Split:

Intervals:

Comments:

Weight: Seasons Best   Personal Best

Post-Training Feeling: Tired   Achy   Proud   Happy   Hard fun

---

Date: Time: AM/PM

Pre-Training Feeling: Weak   Not 100%   Normal   Good   Strong

Distance: SPM:

Time: 500m/Split:

Intervals:

Comments:

Weight: Seasons Best   Personal Best

Post-Training Feeling: Tired   Achy   Proud   Happy   Hard fun

Date: Time: AM/PM

Pre-Training Feeling: Weak   Not 100%   Normal   Good   Strong

Distance: SPM:

Time: 500m/Split:

Intervals:

Comments:

Weight: Seasons Best   Personal Best

Post-Training Feeling: Tired   Achy   Proud   Happy   Hard fun

---

Date: Time: AM/PM

Pre-Training Feeling: Weak   Not 100%   Normal   Good   Strong

Distance: SPM:

Time: 500m/Split:

Intervals:

Comments:

Weight: Seasons Best   Personal Best

Post-Training Feeling: Tired   Achy   Proud   Happy   Hard fun

Date: Time: AM/PM

Pre-Training Feeling: Weak   Not 100%   Normal   Good   Strong

Distance: SPM:

Time: 500m/Split:

Intervals:

Comments:

Weight: Seasons Best   Personal Best

Post-Training Feeling: Tired   Achy   Proud   Happy   Hard fun

---

Date: Time: AM/PM

Pre-Training Feeling: Weak   Not 100%   Normal   Good   Strong

Distance: SPM:

Time: 500m/Split:

Intervals:

Comments:

Weight: Seasons Best   Personal Best

Post-Training Feeling: Tired   Achy   Proud   Happy   Hard fun

Date: Time: AM/PM

Pre-Training Feeling: Weak   Not 100%   Normal   Good   Strong

Distance: SPM:

Time: 500m/Split:

Intervals:

Comments:

Weight: Seasons Best   Personal Best

Post-Training Feeling: Tired   Achy   Proud   Happy   Hard fun

---

Date: Time: AM/PM

Pre-Training Feeling: Weak   Not 100%   Normal   Good   Strong

Distance: SPM:

Time: 500m/Split:

Intervals:

Comments:

Weight: Seasons Best   Personal Best

Post-Training Feeling: Tired   Achy   Proud   Happy   Hard fun

Date: Time: AM/PM

Pre-Training Feeling: Weak   Not 100%   Normal   Good   Strong

Distance: SPM:

Time: 500m/Split:

Intervals:

Comments:

Weight: Seasons Best   Personal Best

Post-Training Feeling: Tired   Achy   Proud   Happy   Hard fun

Date: Time: AM/PM

Pre-Training Feeling: Weak   Not 100%   Normal   Good   Strong

Distance: SPM:

Time: 500m/Split:

Intervals:

Comments:

Weight: Seasons Best   Personal Best

Post-Training Feeling: Tired   Achy   Proud   Happy   Hard fun

Date: Time: AM/PM

Pre-Training Feeling: Weak   Not 100%   Normal   Good   Strong

Distance: SPM:

Time: 500m/Split:

Intervals:

Comments:

Weight: Seasons Best   Personal Best

Post-Training Feeling: Tired   Achy   Proud   Happy   Hard fun

---

Date: Time: AM/PM

Pre-Training Feeling: Weak   Not 100%   Normal   Good   Strong

Distance: SPM:

Time: 500m/Split:

Intervals:

Comments:

Weight: Seasons Best   Personal Best

Post-Training Feeling: Tired   Achy   Proud   Happy   Hard fun

Date: _____ Time: _____ AM/PM

Pre-Training Feeling: Weak   Not 100%   Normal   Good   Strong

Distance: _____   SPM: _____

Time: _____   500m/Split: _____

Intervals: _____

Comments: _____

Weight: _____   Seasons Best _____   Personal Best _____

Post-Training Feeling: Tired   Achy   Proud   Happy   Hard fun

---

Date: [____] Time: [____] AM/PM

Pre-Training Feeling: Weak [ ]   Not 100% [ ]   Normal [ ]   Good [ ]   Strong [ ]

Distance: [____]   SPM: [____]

Time: [____]   500m/Split: [____]

Intervals: [____]

Comments: [____]
[____]

Weight: [__]   Seasons Best [__]   Personal Best [__]

Post-Training Feeling: Tired [ ]   Achy [ ]   Proud [ ]   Happy [ ]   Hard fun [ ]

Date: Time: AM/PM

Pre-Training Feeling: Weak   Not 100%   Normal   Good   Strong

Distance: SPM:

Time: 500m/Split:

Intervals:

Comments:

Weight: Seasons Best   Personal Best

Post-Training Feeling: Tired   Achy   Proud   Happy   Hard fun

---

Date: Time: AM/PM

Pre-Training Feeling: Weak   Not 100%   Normal   Good   Strong

Distance: SPM:

Time: 500m/Split:

Intervals:

Comments:

Weight: Seasons Best   Personal Best

Post-Training Feeling: Tired   Achy   Proud   Happy   Hard fun

Date: Time: AM/PM

Pre-Training Feeling: Weak   Not 100%   Normal   Good   Strong

Distance: SPM:

Time: 500m/Split:

Intervals:

Comments:

Weight: Seasons Best   Personal Best

Post-Training Feeling: Tired   Achy   Proud   Happy   Hard fun

---

Date: [   ]   Time: [   ]   AM/PM

Pre-Training Feeling: Weak ☐   Not 100% ☐   Normal ☐   Good ☐   Strong ☐

Distance: [   ]   SPM: [   ]

Time: [   ]   500m/Split: [   ]

Intervals: [   ]

Comments: [   ]
         [   ]

Weight: [   ]   Seasons Best [   ]   Personal Best [   ]

Post-Training Feeling: Tired ☐   Achy ☐   Proud ☐   Happy ☐   Hard fun ☐

Date: Time: AM/PM

Pre-Training Feeling: Weak   Not 100%   Normal   Good   Strong

Distance: SPM:

Time: 500m/Split:

Intervals:

Comments:

Weight: Seasons Best   Personal Best

Post-Training Feeling: Tired   Achy   Proud   Happy   Hard fun

---

Date: Time: AM/PM

Pre-Training Feeling: Weak   Not 100%   Normal   Good   Strong

Distance: SPM:

Time: 500m/Split:

Intervals:

Comments:

Weight: Seasons Best   Personal Best

Post-Training Feeling: Tired   Achy   Proud   Happy   Hard fun

Date: Time: AM/PM

Pre-Training Feeling: Weak   Not 100%   Normal   Good   Strong

Distance: SPM:

Time: 500m/Split:

Intervals:

Comments:

Weight: Seasons Best   Personal Best

Post-Training Feeling: Tired   Achy   Proud   Happy   Hard fun

---

Date: Time: AM/PM

Pre-Training Feeling: Weak   Not 100%   Normal   Good   Strong

Distance: SPM:

Time: 500m/Split:

Intervals:

Comments:

Weight: Seasons Best   Personal Best

Post-Training Feeling: Tired   Achy   Proud   Happy   Hard fun

Date: Time: AM/PM

Pre-Training Feeling: Weak   Not 100%   Normal   Good   Strong

Distance: SPM:

Time: 500m/Split:

Intervals:

Comments:

Weight: Seasons Best   Personal Best

Post-Training Feeling: Tired   Achy   Proud   Happy   Hard fun

---

Date: Time: AM/PM

Pre-Training Feeling: Weak ☐   Not 100% ☐   Normal ☐   Good ☐   Strong ☐

Distance: SPM:

Time: 500m/Split:

Intervals:

Comments:

Weight: Seasons Best   Personal Best

Post-Training Feeling: Tired ☐   Achy ☐   Proud ☐   Happy ☐   Hard fun ☐

Date: Time: AM/PM

Pre-Training Feeling: Weak   Not 100%   Normal   Good   Strong

Distance: SPM:

Time: 500m/Split:

Intervals:

Comments:

Weight: Seasons Best   Personal Best

Post-Training Feeling: Tired   Achy   Proud   Happy   Hard fun

---

Date: Time: AM/PM

Pre-Training Feeling: Weak   Not 100%   Normal   Good   Strong

Distance: SPM:

Time: 500m/Split:

Intervals:

Comments:

Weight: Seasons Best   Personal Best

Post-Training Feeling: Tired   Achy   Proud   Happy   Hard fun

Date: Time: AM/PM

Pre-Training Feeling: Weak   Not 100%   Normal   Good   Strong

Distance: SPM:

Time: 500m/Split:

Intervals:

Comments:

Weight: Seasons Best   Personal Best

Post-Training Feeling: Tired   Achy   Proud   Happy   Hard fun

---

Date: Time: AM/PM

Pre-Training Feeling: Weak ☐   Not 100% ☐   Normal ☐   Good ☐   Strong ☐

Distance: SPM:

Time: 500m/Split:

Intervals:

Comments:

Weight: Seasons Best   Personal Best

Post-Training Feeling: Tired ☐   Achy ☐   Proud ☐   Happy ☐   Hard fun ☐

Date: Time: AM/PM

Pre-Training Feeling: Weak   Not 100%   Normal   Good   Strong

Distance: SPM:

Time: 500m/Split:

Intervals:

Comments:

Weight: Seasons Best   Personal Best

Post-Training Feeling: Tired   Achy   Proud   Happy   Hard fun

---

Date: Time: AM/PM

Pre-Training Feeling: Weak   Not 100%   Normal   Good   Strong

Distance: SPM:

Time: 500m/Split:

Intervals:

Comments:

Weight: Seasons Best   Personal Best

Post-Training Feeling: Tired   Achy   Proud   Happy   Hard fun

Date: Time: AM/PM

Pre-Training Feeling: Weak   Not 100%   Normal   Good   Strong

Distance: SPM:

Time: 500m/Split:

Intervals:

Comments:

Weight: Seasons Best   Personal Best

Post-Training Feeling: Tired   Achy   Proud   Happy   Hard fun

---

Date: Time: AM/PM

Pre-Training Feeling: Weak   Not 100%   Normal   Good   Strong

Distance: SPM:

Time: 500m/Split:

Intervals:

Comments:

Weight: Seasons Best   Personal Best

Post-Training Feeling: Tired   Achy   Proud   Happy   Hard fun

Date: Time: AM/PM

Pre-Training Feeling: Weak   Not 100%   Normal   Good   Strong

Distance: SPM:

Time: 500m/Split:

Intervals:

Comments:

Weight: Seasons Best   Personal Best

Post-Training Feeling: Tired   Achy   Proud   Happy   Hard fun

Date: Time: AM/PM

Pre-Training Feeling: Weak   Not 100%   Normal   Good   Strong

Distance: SPM:

Time: 500m/Split:

Intervals:

Comments:

Weight: Seasons Best   Personal Best

Post-Training Feeling: Tired   Achy   Proud   Happy   Hard fun

Date: Time: AM/PM

Pre-Training Feeling: Weak   Not 100%   Normal   Good   Strong

Distance: SPM:

Time: 500m/Split:

Intervals:

Comments:

Weight: Seasons Best   Personal Best

Post-Training Feeling: Tired   Achy   Proud   Happy   Hard fun

Date: Time: AM/PM

Pre-Training Feeling: Weak   Not 100%   Normal   Good   Strong

Distance: SPM:

Time: 500m/Split:

Intervals:

Comments:

Weight: Seasons Best   Personal Best

Post-Training Feeling: Tired   Achy   Proud   Happy   Hard fun

Date: Time: AM/PM

Pre-Training Feeling: Weak   Not 100%   Normal   Good   Strong

Distance: SPM:

Time: 500m/Split:

Intervals:

Comments:

Weight: Seasons Best   Personal Best

Post-Training Feeling: Tired   Achy   Proud   Happy   Hard fun

---

Date: Time: AM/PM

Pre-Training Feeling: Weak   Not 100%   Normal   Good   Strong

Distance: SPM:

Time: 500m/Split:

Intervals:

Comments:

Weight: Seasons Best   Personal Best

Post-Training Feeling: Tired   Achy   Proud   Happy   Hard fun

Date: Time: AM/PM

Pre-Training Feeling: Weak   Not 100%   Normal   Good   Strong

Distance: SPM:

Time: 500m/Split:

Intervals:

Comments:

Weight: Seasons Best   Personal Best

Post-Training Feeling: Tired   Achy   Proud   Happy   Hard fun

---

Date: Time: AM/PM

Pre-Training Feeling: Weak   Not 100%   Normal   Good   Strong

Distance: SPM:

Time: 500m/Split:

Intervals:

Comments:

Weight: Seasons Best   Personal Best

Post-Training Feeling: Tired   Achy   Proud   Happy   Hard fun

Date: _____ Time: _____ AM/PM

Pre-Training Feeling: Weak ☐ Not 100% ☐ Normal ☐ Good ☐ Strong ☐

Distance: _____ SPM: _____

Time: _____ 500m/Split: _____

Intervals: _____

Comments: _____

_____

Weight: ___ Seasons Best ___ Personal Best ___

Post-Training Feeling: Tired ☐ Achy ☐ Proud ☐ Happy ☐ Hard fun ☐

Date: _____ Time: _____ AM/PM

Pre-Training Feeling: Weak Not 100% Normal Good Strong

Distance: _____ SPM: _____

Time: _____ 500m/Split: _____

Intervals: _____

Comments: _____

Weight: _____ Seasons Best _____ Personal Best _____

Post-Training Feeling: Tired Achy Proud Happy Hard fun

Date: [_____] Time: [_____] AM/PM

Pre-Training Feeling: Weak ▢ Not 100% ▢ Normal ▢ Good ▢ Strong ▢

Distance: [_____] SPM: [_____]

Time: [_____] 500m/Split: [_____]

Intervals: [_____]

Comments: [_____]
[_____]

Weight: [____] Seasons Best [____] Personal Best [____]

Post-Training Feeling: Tired ▢ Achy ▢ Proud ▢ Happy ▢ Hard fun ▢

Date: Time: AM/PM

Pre-Training Feeling: Weak   Not 100%   Normal   Good   Strong

Distance: SPM:

Time: 500m/Split:

Intervals:

Comments:

Weight: Seasons Best   Personal Best

Post-Training Feeling: Tired   Achy   Proud   Happy   Hard fun

---

Date: Time: AM/PM

Pre-Training Feeling: Weak   Not 100%   Normal   Good   Strong

Distance: SPM:

Time: 500m/Split:

Intervals:

Comments:

Weight: Seasons Best   Personal Best

Post-Training Feeling: Tired   Achy   Proud   Happy   Hard fun

Date: Time: AM/PM

Pre-Training Feeling: Weak   Not 100%   Normal   Good   Strong

Distance: SPM:

Time: 500m/Split:

Intervals:

Comments:

Weight: Seasons Best   Personal Best

Post-Training Feeling: Tired   Achy   Proud   Happy   Hard fun

---

Date: Time: AM/PM

Pre-Training Feeling: Weak   Not 100%   Normal   Good   Strong

Distance: SPM:

Time: 500m/Split:

Intervals:

Comments:

Weight: Seasons Best   Personal Best

Post-Training Feeling: Tired   Achy   Proud   Happy   Hard fun

Date: Time: AM/PM

Pre-Training Feeling: Weak   Not 100%   Normal   Good   Strong

Distance: SPM:

Time: 500m/Split:

Intervals:

Comments:

Weight: Seasons Best   Personal Best

Post-Training Feeling: Tired   Achy   Proud   Happy   Hard fun

---

Date: Time: AM/PM

Pre-Training Feeling: Weak ☐   Not 100% ☐   Normal ☐   Good ☐   Strong ☐

Distance: SPM:

Time: 500m/Split:

Intervals:

Comments:

Weight: Seasons Best   Personal Best

Post-Training Feeling: Tired ☐   Achy ☐   Proud ☐   Happy ☐   Hard fun ☐

Date: Time: AM/PM

Pre-Training Feeling: Weak   Not 100%   Normal   Good   Strong

Distance: SPM:

Time: 500m/Split:

Intervals:

Comments:

Weight: Seasons Best   Personal Best

Post-Training Feeling: Tired   Achy   Proud   Happy   Hard fun

Date: Time: AM/PM

Pre-Training Feeling: Weak   Not 100%   Normal   Good   Strong

Distance: SPM:

Time: 500m/Split:

Intervals:

Comments:

Weight: Seasons Best   Personal Best

Post-Training Feeling: Tired   Achy   Proud   Happy   Hard fun

Date: Time: AM/PM

Pre-Training Feeling: Weak   Not 100%   Normal   Good   Strong

Distance: SPM:

Time: 500m/Split:

Intervals:

Comments:

Weight: Seasons Best   Personal Best

Post-Training Feeling: Tired   Achy   Proud   Happy   Hard fun

Date: Time: AM/PM

Pre-Training Feeling: Weak   Not 100%   Normal   Good   Strong

Distance: SPM:

Time: 500m/Split:

Intervals:

Comments:

Weight: Seasons Best   Personal Best

Post-Training Feeling: Tired   Achy   Proud   Happy   Hard fun

Date: Time: AM/PM

Pre-Training Feeling: Weak   Not 100%   Normal   Good   Strong

Distance: SPM:

Time: 500m/Split:

Intervals:

Comments:

Weight: Seasons Best   Personal Best

Post-Training Feeling: Tired   Achy   Proud   Happy   Hard fun

---

Date: Time: AM/PM

Pre-Training Feeling: Weak ☐   Not 100% ☐   Normal ☐   Good ☐   Strong ☐

Distance: SPM:

Time: 500m/Split:

Intervals:

Comments:

Weight: Seasons Best   Personal Best

Post-Training Feeling: Tired ☐   Achy ☐   Proud ☐   Happy ☐   Hard fun ☐

Date: Time: AM/PM

Pre-Training Feeling: Weak   Not 100%   Normal   Good   Strong

Distance: SPM:

Time: 500m/Split:

Intervals:

Comments:

Weight: Seasons Best   Personal Best

Post-Training Feeling: Tired   Achy   Proud   Happy   Hard fun

---

Date: Time: AM/PM

Pre-Training Feeling: Weak   Not 100%   Normal   Good   Strong

Distance: SPM:

Time: 500m/Split:

Intervals:

Comments:

Weight: Seasons Best   Personal Best

Post-Training Feeling: Tired   Achy   Proud   Happy   Hard fun

Date: Time: AM/PM

Pre-Training Feeling: Weak   Not 100%   Normal   Good   Strong

Distance: SPM:

Time: 500m/Split:

Intervals:

Comments:

Weight: Seasons Best   Personal Best

Post-Training Feeling: Tired   Achy   Proud   Happy   Hard fun

---

Date: Time: AM/PM

Pre-Training Feeling: Weak   Not 100%   Normal   Good   Strong

Distance: SPM:

Time: 500m/Split:

Intervals:

Comments:

Weight: Seasons Best   Personal Best

Post-Training Feeling: Tired   Achy   Proud   Happy   Hard fun

Date: Time: AM/PM

Pre-Training Feeling: Weak   Not 100%   Normal   Good   Strong

Distance: SPM:

Time: 500m/Split:

Intervals:

Comments:

Weight: Seasons Best   Personal Best

Post-Training Feeling: Tired   Achy   Proud   Happy   Hard fun

---

Date: Time: AM/PM

Pre-Training Feeling: Weak   Not 100%   Normal   Good   Strong

Distance: SPM:

Time: 500m/Split:

Intervals:

Comments:

Weight: Seasons Best   Personal Best

Post-Training Feeling: Tired   Achy   Proud   Happy   Hard fun

Date: Time: AM/PM

Pre-Training Feeling: Weak   Not 100%   Normal   Good   Strong

Distance: SPM:

Time: 500m/Split:

Intervals:

Comments:

Weight: Seasons Best   Personal Best

Post-Training Feeling: Tired   Achy   Proud   Happy   Hard fun

---

Date: Time: AM/PM

Pre-Training Feeling: Weak   Not 100%   Normal   Good   Strong

Distance: SPM:

Time: 500m/Split:

Intervals:

Comments:

Weight: Seasons Best   Personal Best

Post-Training Feeling: Tired   Achy   Proud   Happy   Hard fun

Date: Time: AM/PM

Pre-Training Feeling: Weak   Not 100%   Normal   Good   Strong

Distance: SPM:

Time: 500m/Split:

Intervals:

Comments:

Weight: Seasons Best   Personal Best

Post-Training Feeling: Tired   Achy   Proud   Happy   Hard fun

Date: Time: AM/PM

Pre-Training Feeling: Weak   Not 100%   Normal   Good   Strong

Distance: SPM:

Time: 500m/Split:

Intervals:

Comments:

Weight: Seasons Best   Personal Best

Post-Training Feeling: Tired   Achy   Proud   Happy   Hard fun

Date: Time: AM/PM

Pre-Training Feeling: Weak   Not 100%   Normal   Good   Strong

Distance: SPM:

Time: 500m/Split:

Intervals:

Comments:

Weight: Seasons Best   Personal Best

Post-Training Feeling: Tired   Achy   Proud   Happy   Hard fun

---

Date: Time: AM/PM

Pre-Training Feeling: Weak   Not 100%   Normal   Good   Strong

Distance: SPM:

Time: 500m/Split:

Intervals:

Comments:

Weight: Seasons Best   Personal Best

Post-Training Feeling: Tired   Achy   Proud   Happy   Hard fun

Date: Time: AM/PM

Pre-Training Feeling: Weak   Not 100%   Normal   Good   Strong

Distance: SPM:

Time: 500m/Split:

Intervals:

Comments:

Weight: Seasons Best   Personal Best

Post-Training Feeling: Tired   Achy   Proud   Happy   Hard fun

Date: Time: AM/PM

Pre-Training Feeling: Weak   Not 100%   Normal   Good   Strong

Distance: SPM:

Time: 500m/Split:

Intervals:

Comments:

Weight: Seasons Best   Personal Best

Post-Training Feeling: Tired   Achy   Proud   Happy   Hard fun

Date: Time: AM/PM

Pre-Training Feeling: Weak   Not 100%   Normal   Good   Strong

Distance: SPM:

Time: 500m/Split:

Intervals:

Comments:

Weight: Seasons Best   Personal Best

Post-Training Feeling: Tired   Achy   Proud   Happy   Hard fun

---

Date: Time: AM/PM

Pre-Training Feeling: Weak   Not 100%   Normal   Good   Strong

Distance: SPM:

Time: 500m/Split:

Intervals:

Comments:

Weight: Seasons Best   Personal Best

Post-Training Feeling: Tired   Achy   Proud   Happy   Hard fun

Date: Time: AM/PM

Pre-Training Feeling: Weak   Not 100%   Normal   Good   Strong

Distance: SPM:

Time: 500m/Split:

Intervals:

Comments:

Weight: Seasons Best   Personal Best

Post-Training Feeling: Tired   Achy   Proud   Happy   Hard fun

Date: Time: AM/PM

Pre-Training Feeling: Weak ☐   Not 100% ☐   Normal ☐   Good ☐   Strong ☐

Distance: SPM:

Time: 500m/Split:

Intervals:

Comments:

Weight: Seasons Best   Personal Best

Post-Training Feeling: Tired ☐   Achy ☐   Proud ☐   Happy ☐   Hard fun ☐

Date: Time: AM/PM

Pre-Training Feeling: Weak   Not 100%   Normal   Good   Strong

Distance: SPM:

Time: 500m/Split:

Intervals:

Comments:

Weight: Seasons Best   Personal Best

Post-Training Feeling: Tired   Achy   Proud   Happy   Hard fun

Date: Time: AM/PM

Pre-Training Feeling: Weak   Not 100%   Normal   Good   Strong

Distance: SPM:

Time: 500m/Split:

Intervals:

Comments:

Weight: Seasons Best   Personal Best

Post-Training Feeling: Tired   Achy   Proud   Happy   Hard fun

Date: Time: AM/PM

Pre-Training Feeling: Weak   Not 100%   Normal   Good   Strong

Distance: SPM:

Time: 500m/Split:

Intervals:

Comments:

Weight: Seasons Best   Personal Best

Post-Training Feeling: Tired   Achy   Proud   Happy   Hard fun

---

Date: Time: AM/PM

Pre-Training Feeling: Weak   Not 100%   Normal   Good   Strong

Distance: SPM:

Time: 500m/Split:

Intervals:

Comments:

Weight: Seasons Best   Personal Best

Post-Training Feeling: Tired   Achy   Proud   Happy   Hard fun

Date: Time: AM/PM

Pre-Training Feeling: Weak   Not 100%   Normal   Good   Strong

Distance: SPM:

Time: 500m/Split:

Intervals:

Comments:

Weight: Seasons Best   Personal Best

Post-Training Feeling: Tired   Achy   Proud   Happy   Hard fun

---

Date: Time: AM/PM

Pre-Training Feeling: Weak   Not 100%   Normal   Good   Strong

Distance: SPM:

Time: 500m/Split:

Intervals:

Comments:

Weight: Seasons Best   Personal Best

Post-Training Feeling: Tired   Achy   Proud   Happy   Hard fun

Date: Time: AM/PM

Pre-Training Feeling: Weak   Not 100%   Normal   Good   Strong

Distance: SPM:

Time: 500m/Split:

Intervals:

Comments:

Weight: Seasons Best   Personal Best

Post-Training Feeling: Tired   Achy   Proud   Happy   Hard fun

---

Date: Time: AM/PM

Pre-Training Feeling: Weak   Not 100%   Normal   Good   Strong

Distance: SPM:

Time: 500m/Split:

Intervals:

Comments:

Weight: Seasons Best   Personal Best

Post-Training Feeling: Tired   Achy   Proud   Happy   Hard fun

Date: Time: AM/PM

Pre-Training Feeling: Weak   Not 100%   Normal   Good   Strong

Distance: SPM:

Time: 500m/Split:

Intervals:

Comments:

Weight: Seasons Best   Personal Best

Post-Training Feeling: Tired   Achy   Proud   Happy   Hard fun

---

Date: Time: AM/PM

Pre-Training Feeling: Weak   Not 100%   Normal   Good   Strong

Distance: SPM:

Time: 500m/Split:

Intervals:

Comments:

Weight: Seasons Best   Personal Best

Post-Training Feeling: Tired   Achy   Proud   Happy   Hard fun

Date: _____ Time: _____ AM/PM

Pre-Training Feeling: Weak   Not 100%   Normal   Good   Strong

Distance: _____ SPM: _____

Time: _____ 500m/Split: _____

Intervals: _____

Comments: _____

Weight: _____ Seasons Best   Personal Best

Post-Training Feeling: Tired   Achy   Proud   Happy   Hard fun

---

Date: [ ] Time: [ ] AM/PM

Pre-Training Feeling: Weak [ ] Not 100% [ ] Normal [ ] Good [ ] Strong [ ]

Distance: [ ] SPM: [ ]

Time: [ ] 500m/Split: [ ]

Intervals: [ ]

Comments: [ ]

Weight: [ ] Seasons Best [ ] Personal Best [ ]

Post-Training Feeling: Tired [ ] Achy [ ] Proud [ ] Happy [ ] Hard fun [ ]

Date: Time: AM/PM

Pre-Training Feeling: Weak   Not 100%   Normal   Good   Strong

Distance: SPM:

Time: 500m/Split:

Intervals:

Comments:

Weight: Seasons Best   Personal Best

Post-Training Feeling: Tired   Achy   Proud   Happy   Hard fun

---

Date: Time: AM/PM

Pre-Training Feeling: Weak   Not 100%   Normal   Good   Strong

Distance: SPM:

Time: 500m/Split:

Intervals:

Comments:

Weight: Seasons Best   Personal Best

Post-Training Feeling: Tired   Achy   Proud   Happy   Hard fun

Date: Time: AM/PM

Pre-Training Feeling: Weak   Not 100%   Normal   Good   Strong

Distance: SPM:

Time: 500m/Split:

Intervals:

Comments:

Weight: Seasons Best   Personal Best

Post-Training Feeling: Tired   Achy   Proud   Happy   Hard fun

---

Date: Time: AM/PM

Pre-Training Feeling: Weak   Not 100%   Normal   Good   Strong

Distance: SPM:

Time: 500m/Split:

Intervals:

Comments:

Weight: Seasons Best   Personal Best

Post-Training Feeling: Tired   Achy   Proud   Happy   Hard fun

Date: Time: AM/PM

Pre-Training Feeling: Weak   Not 100%   Normal   Good   Strong

Distance: SPM:

Time: 500m/Split:

Intervals:

Comments:

Weight: Seasons Best   Personal Best

Post-Training Feeling: Tired   Achy   Proud   Happy   Hard fun

---

Date: Time: AM/PM

Pre-Training Feeling: Weak   Not 100%   Normal   Good   Strong

Distance: SPM:

Time: 500m/Split:

Intervals:

Comments:

Weight: Seasons Best   Personal Best

Post-Training Feeling: Tired   Achy   Proud   Happy   Hard fun

Date: Time: AM/PM

Pre-Training Feeling: Weak   Not 100%   Normal   Good   Strong

Distance: SPM:

Time: 500m/Split:

Intervals:

Comments:

Weight: Seasons Best   Personal Best

Post-Training Feeling: Tired   Achy   Proud   Happy   Hard fun

Date: Time: AM/PM

Pre-Training Feeling: Weak   Not 100%   Normal   Good   Strong

Distance: SPM:

Time: 500m/Split:

Intervals:

Comments:

Weight: Seasons Best   Personal Best

Post-Training Feeling: Tired   Achy   Proud   Happy   Hard fun

Date: Time: AM/PM

Pre-Training Feeling: Weak   Not 100%   Normal   Good   Strong

Distance: SPM:

Time: 500m/Split:

Intervals:

Comments:

Weight: Seasons Best   Personal Best

Post-Training Feeling: Tired   Achy   Proud   Happy   Hard fun

---

Date: Time: AM/PM

Pre-Training Feeling: Weak   Not 100%   Normal   Good   Strong

Distance: SPM:

Time: 500m/Split:

Intervals:

Comments:

Weight: Seasons Best   Personal Best

Post-Training Feeling: Tired   Achy   Proud   Happy   Hard fun

Date: Time: AM/PM

Pre-Training Feeling: Weak   Not 100%   Normal   Good   Strong

Distance: SPM:

Time: 500m/Split:

Intervals:

Comments:

Weight: Seasons Best   Personal Best

Post-Training Feeling: Tired   Achy   Proud   Happy   Hard fun

---

Date: Time: AM/PM

Pre-Training Feeling: Weak   Not 100%   Normal   Good   Strong

Distance: SPM:

Time: 500m/Split:

Intervals:

Comments:

Weight: Seasons Best   Personal Best

Post-Training Feeling: Tired   Achy   Proud   Happy   Hard fun

Date: Time: AM/PM

Pre-Training Feeling: Weak   Not 100%   Normal   Good   Strong

Distance: SPM:

Time: 500m/Split:

Intervals:

Comments:

Weight: Seasons Best   Personal Best

Post-Training Feeling: Tired   Achy   Proud   Happy   Hard fun

---

Date: Time: AM/PM

Pre-Training Feeling: Weak   Not 100%   Normal   Good   Strong

Distance: SPM:

Time: 500m/Split:

Intervals:

Comments:

Weight: Seasons Best   Personal Best

Post-Training Feeling: Tired   Achy   Proud   Happy   Hard fun

Date: Time: AM/PM

Pre-Training Feeling: Weak   Not 100%   Normal   Good   Strong

Distance: SPM:

Time: 500m/Split:

Intervals:

Comments:

Weight: Seasons Best   Personal Best

Post-Training Feeling: Tired   Achy   Proud   Happy   Hard fun

---

Date: Time: AM/PM

Pre-Training Feeling: Weak   Not 100%   Normal   Good   Strong

Distance: SPM:

Time: 500m/Split:

Intervals:

Comments:

Weight: Seasons Best   Personal Best

Post-Training Feeling: Tired   Achy   Proud   Happy   Hard fun

Date: Time: AM/PM

Pre-Training Feeling: Weak   Not 100%   Normal   Good   Strong

Distance: SPM:

Time: 500m/Split:

Intervals:

Comments:

Weight: Seasons Best   Personal Best

Post-Training Feeling: Tired   Achy   Proud   Happy   Hard fun

---

Date: Time: AM/PM

Pre-Training Feeling: Weak   Not 100%   Normal   Good   Strong

Distance: SPM:

Time: 500m/Split:

Intervals:

Comments:

Weight: Seasons Best   Personal Best

Post-Training Feeling: Tired   Achy   Proud   Happy   Hard fun

Date: Time: AM/PM

Pre-Training Feeling: Weak   Not 100%   Normal   Good   Strong

Distance: SPM:

Time: 500m/Split:

Intervals:

Comments:

Weight: Seasons Best   Personal Best

Post-Training Feeling: Tired   Achy   Proud   Happy   Hard fun

Date: Time: AM/PM

Pre-Training Feeling: Weak   Not 100%   Normal   Good   Strong

Distance: SPM:

Time: 500m/Split:

Intervals:

Comments:

Weight: Seasons Best   Personal Best

Post-Training Feeling: Tired   Achy   Proud   Happy   Hard fun

Date: Time: AM/PM

Pre-Training Feeling: Weak   Not 100%   Normal   Good   Strong

Distance: SPM:

Time: 500m/Split:

Intervals:

Comments:

Weight: Seasons Best   Personal Best

Post-Training Feeling: Tired   Achy   Proud   Happy   Hard fun

---

Date: Time: AM/PM

Pre-Training Feeling: Weak   Not 100%   Normal   Good   Strong

Distance: SPM:

Time: 500m/Split:

Intervals:

Comments:

Weight: Seasons Best   Personal Best

Post-Training Feeling: Tired   Achy   Proud   Happy   Hard fun

Date: _____ Time: _____ AM/PM

Pre-Training Feeling: Weak   Not 100%   Normal   Good   Strong

Distance: _____ SPM: _____

Time: _____ 500m/Split: _____

Intervals: _____

Comments: _____

Weight: _____ Seasons Best   Personal Best

Post-Training Feeling: Tired   Achy   Proud   Happy   Hard fun

---

Date: [____] Time: [____] AM/PM

Pre-Training Feeling: Weak ☐ Not 100% ☐ Normal ☐ Good ☐ Strong ☐

Distance: [____] SPM: [____]

Time: [____] 500m/Split: [____]

Intervals: [____]

Comments: [____]

Weight: [____] Seasons Best ☐ Personal Best ☐

Post-Training Feeling: Tired ☐ Achy ☐ Proud ☐ Happy ☐ Hard fun ☐

Date: Time: AM/PM

Pre-Training Feeling: Weak   Not 100%   Normal   Good   Strong

Distance: SPM:

Time: 500m/Split:

Intervals:

Comments:

Weight: Seasons Best   Personal Best

Post-Training Feeling: Tired   Achy   Proud   Happy   Hard fun

---

Date: Time: AM/PM

Pre-Training Feeling: Weak   Not 100%   Normal   Good   Strong

Distance: SPM:

Time: 500m/Split:

Intervals:

Comments:

Weight: Seasons Best   Personal Best

Post-Training Feeling: Tired   Achy   Proud   Happy   Hard fun

Date: Time: AM/PM

Pre-Training Feeling: Weak   Not 100%   Normal   Good   Strong

Distance: SPM:

Time: 500m/Split:

Intervals:

Comments:

Weight: Seasons Best   Personal Best

Post-Training Feeling: Tired   Achy   Proud   Happy   Hard fun

---

Date: Time: AM/PM

Pre-Training Feeling: Weak ☐   Not 100% ☐   Normal ☐   Good ☐   Strong ☐

Distance: SPM:

Time: 500m/Split:

Intervals:

Comments:

Weight: Seasons Best   Personal Best

Post-Training Feeling: Tired ☐   Achy ☐   Proud ☐   Happy ☐   Hard fun ☐

Date: Time: AM/PM

Pre-Training Feeling: Weak   Not 100%   Normal   Good   Strong

Distance: SPM:

Time: 500m/Split:

Intervals:

Comments:

Weight: Seasons Best   Personal Best

Post-Training Feeling: Tired   Achy   Proud   Happy   Hard fun

---

Date: Time: AM/PM

Pre-Training Feeling: Weak   Not 100%   Normal   Good   Strong

Distance: SPM:

Time: 500m/Split:

Intervals:

Comments:

Weight: Seasons Best   Personal Best

Post-Training Feeling: Tired   Achy   Proud   Happy   Hard fun

Date: Time: AM/PM

Pre-Training Feeling: Weak   Not 100%   Normal   Good   Strong

Distance: SPM:

Time: 500m/Split:

Intervals:

Comments:

Weight: Seasons Best   Personal Best

Post-Training Feeling: Tired   Achy   Proud   Happy   Hard fun

Date: Time: AM/PM

Pre-Training Feeling: Weak   Not 100%   Normal   Good   Strong

Distance: SPM:

Time: 500m/Split:

Intervals:

Comments:

Weight: Seasons Best   Personal Best

Post-Training Feeling: Tired   Achy   Proud   Happy   Hard fun

Date: Time: AM/PM

Pre-Training Feeling: Weak   Not 100%   Normal   Good   Strong

Distance: SPM:

Time: 500m/Split:

Intervals:

Comments:

Weight: Seasons Best   Personal Best

Post-Training Feeling: Tired   Achy   Proud   Happy   Hard fun

---

Date: Time: AM/PM

Pre-Training Feeling: Weak   Not 100%   Normal   Good   Strong

Distance: SPM:

Time: 500m/Split:

Intervals:

Comments:

Weight: Seasons Best   Personal Best

Post-Training Feeling: Tired   Achy   Proud   Happy   Hard fun

Date: Time: AM/PM

Pre-Training Feeling: Weak   Not 100%   Normal   Good   Strong

Distance: SPM:

Time: 500m/Split:

Intervals:

Comments:

Weight: Seasons Best   Personal Best

Post-Training Feeling: Tired   Achy   Proud   Happy   Hard fun

---

Date: [ ]   Time: [ ]   AM/PM

Pre-Training Feeling: Weak [ ] Not 100% [ ] Normal [ ] Good [ ] Strong [ ]

Distance: [ ]   SPM: [ ]

Time: [ ]   500m/Split: [ ]

Intervals: [ ]

Comments: [ ]
[ ]

Weight: [ ]   Seasons Best [ ]   Personal Best [ ]

Post-Training Feeling: Tired [ ] Achy [ ] Proud [ ] Happy [ ] Hard fun [ ]

Date: Time: AM/PM

Pre-Training Feeling: Weak   Not 100%   Normal   Good   Strong

Distance: SPM:

Time: 500m/Split:

Intervals:

Comments:

Weight: Seasons Best   Personal Best

Post-Training Feeling: Tired   Achy   Proud   Happy   Hard fun

---

Date: Time: AM/PM

Pre-Training Feeling: Weak   Not 100%   Normal   Good   Strong

Distance: SPM:

Time: 500m/Split:

Intervals:

Comments:

Weight: Seasons Best   Personal Best

Post-Training Feeling: Tired   Achy   Proud   Happy   Hard fun

Date: _____ Time: _____ AM/PM

Pre-Training Feeling: Weak   Not 100%   Normal   Good   Strong

Distance: _____ SPM: _____

Time: _____ 500m/Split: _____

Intervals: _____

Comments: _____

Weight: _____ Seasons Best   Personal Best

Post-Training Feeling: Tired   Achy   Proud   Happy   Hard fun

---

Date: [____] Time: [____] AM/PM

Pre-Training Feeling: Weak [ ]   Not 100% [ ]   Normal [ ]   Good [ ]   Strong [ ]

Distance: [____] SPM: [____]

Time: [____] 500m/Split: [____]

Intervals: [____]

Comments: [____]

[____]

Weight: [ ]   Seasons Best [ ]   Personal Best [ ]

Post-Training Feeling: Tired [ ]   Achy [ ]   Proud [ ]   Happy [ ]   Hard fun [ ]

Date: Time: AM/PM

Pre-Training Feeling: Weak   Not 100%   Normal   Good   Strong

Distance: SPM:

Time: 500m/Split:

Intervals:

Comments:

Weight: Seasons Best   Personal Best

Post-Training Feeling: Tired   Achy   Proud   Happy   Hard fun

---

Date: Time: AM/PM

Pre-Training Feeling: Weak   Not 100%   Normal   Good   Strong

Distance: SPM:

Time: 500m/Split:

Intervals:

Comments:

Weight: Seasons Best   Personal Best

Post-Training Feeling: Tired   Achy   Proud   Happy   Hard fun

Date: Time: AM/PM

Pre-Training Feeling: Weak   Not 100%   Normal   Good   Strong

Distance: SPM:

Time: 500m/Split:

Intervals:

Comments:

Weight: Seasons Best   Personal Best

Post-Training Feeling: Tired   Achy   Proud   Happy   Hard fun

---

Date: Time: AM/PM

Pre-Training Feeling: Weak □   Not 100% □   Normal □   Good □   Strong □

Distance: SPM:

Time: 500m/Split:

Intervals:

Comments:

Weight: Seasons Best   Personal Best

Post-Training Feeling: Tired □   Achy □   Proud □   Happy □   Hard fun □

Date: Time: AM/PM

Pre-Training Feeling: Weak   Not 100%   Normal   Good   Strong

Distance: SPM:

Time: 500m/Split:

Intervals:

Comments:

Weight: Seasons Best   Personal Best

Post-Training Feeling: Tired   Achy   Proud   Happy   Hard fun

---

Date: Time: AM/PM

Pre-Training Feeling: Weak   Not 100%   Normal   Good   Strong

Distance: SPM:

Time: 500m/Split:

Intervals:

Comments:

Weight: Seasons Best   Personal Best

Post-Training Feeling: Tired   Achy   Proud   Happy   Hard fun

Date: Time: AM/PM

Pre-Training Feeling: Weak   Not 100%   Normal   Good   Strong

Distance: SPM:

Time: 500m/Split:

Intervals:

Comments:

Weight: Seasons Best   Personal Best

Post-Training Feeling: Tired   Achy   Proud   Happy   Hard fun

---

Date: Time: AM/PM

Pre-Training Feeling: Weak ☐   Not 100% ☐   Normal ☐   Good ☐   Strong ☐

Distance: SPM:

Time: 500m/Split:

Intervals:

Comments:

Weight: Seasons Best   Personal Best

Post-Training Feeling: Tired ☐   Achy ☐   Proud ☐   Happy ☐   Hard fun ☐

Date: Time: AM/PM

Pre-Training Feeling: Weak   Not 100%   Normal   Good   Strong

Distance: SPM:

Time: 500m/Split:

Intervals:

Comments:

Weight: Seasons Best   Personal Best

Post-Training Feeling: Tired   Achy   Proud   Happy   Hard fun

---

Date: Time: AM/PM

Pre-Training Feeling: Weak   Not 100%   Normal   Good   Strong

Distance: SPM:

Time: 500m/Split:

Intervals:

Comments:

Weight: Seasons Best   Personal Best

Post-Training Feeling: Tired   Achy   Proud   Happy   Hard fun

Date: Time: AM/PM

Pre-Training Feeling: Weak   Not 100%   Normal   Good   Strong

Distance: SPM:

Time: 500m/Split:

Intervals:

Comments:

Weight: Seasons Best   Personal Best

Post-Training Feeling: Tired   Achy   Proud   Happy   Hard fun

---

Date: Time: AM/PM

Pre-Training Feeling: Weak [ ]   Not 100% [ ]   Normal [ ]   Good [ ]   Strong [ ]

Distance: SPM:

Time: 500m/Split:

Intervals:

Comments:

Weight: Seasons Best   Personal Best

Post-Training Feeling: Tired [ ]   Achy [ ]   Proud [ ]   Happy [ ]   Hard fun [ ]

Date: Time: AM/PM

Pre-Training Feeling: Weak   Not 100%   Normal   Good   Strong

Distance: SPM:

Time: 500m/Split:

Intervals:

Comments:

Weight: Seasons Best   Personal Best

Post-Training Feeling: Tired   Achy   Proud   Happy   Hard fun

---

Date: Time: AM/PM

Pre-Training Feeling: Weak   Not 100%   Normal   Good   Strong

Distance: SPM:

Time: 500m/Split:

Intervals:

Comments:

Weight: Seasons Best   Personal Best

Post-Training Feeling: Tired   Achy   Proud   Happy   Hard fun

Date: Time: AM/PM

Pre-Training Feeling: Weak   Not 100%   Normal   Good   Strong

Distance: SPM:

Time: 500m/Split:

Intervals:

Comments:

Weight: Seasons Best   Personal Best

Post-Training Feeling: Tired   Achy   Proud   Happy   Hard fun

---

Date: Time: AM/PM

Pre-Training Feeling: Weak   Not 100%   Normal   Good   Strong

Distance: SPM:

Time: 500m/Split:

Intervals:

Comments:

Weight: Seasons Best   Personal Best

Post-Training Feeling: Tired   Achy   Proud   Happy   Hard fun

Date: Time: AM/PM

Pre-Training Feeling: Weak   Not 100%   Normal   Good   Strong

Distance: SPM:

Time: 500m/Split:

Intervals:

Comments:

Weight: Seasons Best   Personal Best

Post-Training Feeling: Tired   Achy   Proud   Happy   Hard fun

Date: Time: AM/PM

Pre-Training Feeling: Weak   Not 100%   Normal   Good   Strong

Distance: SPM:

Time: 500m/Split:

Intervals:

Comments:

Weight: Seasons Best   Personal Best

Post-Training Feeling: Tired   Achy   Proud   Happy   Hard fun

Date: _____ Time: _____ AM/PM

Pre-Training Feeling: Weak   Not 100%   Normal   Good   Strong

Distance: _____ SPM: _____

Time: _____ 500m/Split: _____

Intervals: _____

Comments: _____

Weight: _____ Seasons Best   Personal Best

Post-Training Feeling: Tired   Achy   Proud   Happy   Hard fun

---

Date: [_____] Time: [_____] AM/PM

Pre-Training Feeling: Weak [ ]   Not 100% [ ]   Normal [ ]   Good [ ]   Strong [ ]

Distance: [_____] SPM: [_____]

Time: [_____] 500m/Split: [_____]

Intervals: [_____]

Comments: [_____]

[_____]

Weight: [____] Seasons Best [ ]   Personal Best [ ]

Post-Training Feeling: Tired [ ]   Achy [ ]   Proud [ ]   Happy [ ]   Hard fun [ ]

Date: _____ Time: _____ AM/PM

Pre-Training Feeling: Weak   Not 100%   Normal   Good   Strong

Distance: _____ SPM: _____

Time: _____ 500m/Split: _____

Intervals: _____

Comments: _____

Weight: _____ Seasons Best _____ Personal Best _____

Post-Training Feeling: Tired   Achy   Proud   Happy   Hard fun

---

Date: [_____] Time: [_____] AM/PM

Pre-Training Feeling: Weak ☐ Not 100% ☐ Normal ☐ Good ☐ Strong ☐

Distance: [_____] SPM: [_____]

Time: [_____] 500m/Split: [_____]

Intervals: [_____]

Comments: [_____]

[_____]

Weight: [_____] Seasons Best [_____] Personal Best [_____]

Post-Training Feeling: Tired ☐ Achy ☐ Proud ☐ Happy ☐ Hard fun ☐

Date: Time: AM/PM

Pre-Training Feeling: Weak   Not 100%   Normal   Good   Strong

Distance: SPM:

Time: 500m/Split:

Intervals:

Comments:

Weight: Seasons Best   Personal Best

Post-Training Feeling: Tired   Achy   Proud   Happy   Hard fun

---

Date: Time: AM/PM

Pre-Training Feeling: Weak   Not 100%   Normal   Good   Strong

Distance: SPM:

Time: 500m/Split:

Intervals:

Comments:

Weight: Seasons Best   Personal Best

Post-Training Feeling: Tired   Achy   Proud   Happy   Hard fun

Date: _____ Time: _____ AM/PM

Pre-Training Feeling: Weak   Not 100%   Normal   Good   Strong

Distance: _____ SPM: _____

Time: _____ 500m/Split: _____

Intervals: _____

Comments: _____

Weight: _____ Seasons Best   Personal Best

Post-Training Feeling: Tired   Achy   Proud   Happy   Hard fun

---

Date: [_____]   Time: [_____]   AM/PM

Pre-Training Feeling: Weak [ ]   Not 100% [ ]   Normal [ ]   Good [ ]   Strong [ ]

Distance: [_____]   SPM: [_____]

Time: [_____]   500m/Split: [_____]

Intervals: [_____]

Comments: [_____]
[_____]

Weight: [__]   Seasons Best [__]   Personal Best [__]

Post-Training Feeling: Tired [ ]   Achy [ ]   Proud [ ]   Happy [ ]   Hard fun [ ]

Date: Time: AM/PM

Pre-Training Feeling: Weak   Not 100%   Normal   Good   Strong

Distance: SPM:

Time: 500m/Split:

Intervals:

Comments:

Weight: Seasons Best   Personal Best

Post-Training Feeling: Tired   Achy   Proud   Happy   Hard fun

Date: Time: AM/PM

Pre-Training Feeling: Weak   Not 100%   Normal   Good   Strong

Distance: SPM:

Time: 500m/Split:

Intervals:

Comments:

Weight: Seasons Best   Personal Best

Post-Training Feeling: Tired   Achy   Proud   Happy   Hard fun

Date: Time: AM/PM

Pre-Training Feeling: Weak   Not 100%   Normal   Good   Strong

Distance: SPM:

Time: 500m/Split:

Intervals:

Comments:

Weight: Seasons Best   Personal Best

Post-Training Feeling: Tired   Achy   Proud   Happy   Hard fun

---

Date: Time: AM/PM

Pre-Training Feeling: Weak   Not 100%   Normal   Good   Strong

Distance: SPM:

Time: 500m/Split:

Intervals:

Comments:

Weight: Seasons Best   Personal Best

Post-Training Feeling: Tired   Achy   Proud   Happy   Hard fun

Date: _____ Time: _____ AM/PM

Pre-Training Feeling: Weak   Not 100%   Normal   Good   Strong

Distance: _____ SPM: _____

Time: _____ 500m/Split: _____

Intervals: _____

Comments: _____

Weight: _____ Seasons Best _____ Personal Best _____

Post-Training Feeling: Tired   Achy   Proud   Happy   Hard fun

---

Date: [_____] Time: [_____] AM/PM

Pre-Training Feeling: Weak ☐ Not 100% ☐ Normal ☐ Good ☐ Strong ☐

Distance: [_____] SPM: [_____]

Time: [_____] 500m/Split: [_____]

Intervals: [_____]

Comments: [_____]
[_____]

Weight: [__] Seasons Best [__] Personal Best [__]

Post-Training Feeling: Tired ☐ Achy ☐ Proud ☐ Happy ☐ Hard fun ☐

Date: Time: AM/PM

Pre-Training Feeling: Weak   Not 100%   Normal   Good   Strong

Distance: SPM:

Time: 500m/Split:

Intervals:

Comments:

Weight: Seasons Best   Personal Best

Post-Training Feeling: Tired   Achy   Proud   Happy   Hard fun

---

Date: Time: AM/PM

Pre-Training Feeling: Weak   Not 100%   Normal   Good   Strong

Distance: SPM:

Time: 500m/Split:

Intervals:

Comments:

Weight: Seasons Best   Personal Best

Post-Training Feeling: Tired   Achy   Proud   Happy   Hard fun

Date: Time: AM/PM

Pre-Training Feeling: Weak   Not 100%   Normal   Good   Strong

Distance: SPM:

Time: 500m/Split:

Intervals:

Comments:

Weight: Seasons Best   Personal Best

Post-Training Feeling: Tired   Achy   Proud   Happy   Hard fun

---

Date: Time: AM/PM

Pre-Training Feeling: Weak ☐   Not 100% ☐   Normal ☐   Good ☐   Strong ☐

Distance: SPM:

Time: 500m/Split:

Intervals:

Comments:

Weight: ☐   Seasons Best ☐   Personal Best ☐

Post-Training Feeling: Tired ☐   Achy ☐   Proud ☐   Happy ☐   Hard fun ☐

Date: Time: AM/PM

Pre-Training Feeling: Weak   Not 100%   Normal   Good   Strong

Distance: SPM:

Time: 500m/Split:

Intervals:

Comments:

Weight: Seasons Best   Personal Best

Post-Training Feeling: Tired   Achy   Proud   Happy   Hard fun

---

Date: Time: AM/PM

Pre-Training Feeling: Weak   Not 100%   Normal   Good   Strong

Distance: SPM:

Time: 500m/Split:

Intervals:

Comments:

Weight: Seasons Best   Personal Best

Post-Training Feeling: Tired   Achy   Proud   Happy   Hard fun

Date: Time: AM/PM

Pre-Training Feeling: Weak   Not 100%   Normal   Good   Strong

Distance: SPM:

Time: 500m/Split:

Intervals:

Comments:

Weight: Seasons Best   Personal Best

Post-Training Feeling: Tired   Achy   Proud   Happy   Hard fun

---

Date: Time: AM/PM

Pre-Training Feeling: Weak   Not 100%   Normal   Good   Strong

Distance: SPM:

Time: 500m/Split:

Intervals:

Comments:

Weight: Seasons Best   Personal Best

Post-Training Feeling: Tired   Achy   Proud   Happy   Hard fun

Notes

Notes

Notes

Notes

Notes

Printed in Great Britain
by Amazon

47762992R00069